CHILD DEVELOPMENT
AND MORE...

Birth to Twelve Years

CHILD DEVELOPMENT AND MORE ...

Birth to Twelve Years

by

Katie M. Bille

Orange Tree Publications
Cross Plains, Wisconsin

Published by   Orange Tree Publications
               P.O. Box 70
               Cross Plains, WI 53528

Technical Editing and Layout by Editing Services
                               Madison, WI 53717

Printed by Omni Press
           Madison, WI 53704

ISBN 0-9745973-0-9

Dedication

First and foremost, I would like to thank God for all his blessings and strength throughout my life.

I wish to express my gratitude to my husband Dale and our two daughters, Camarie and Kensey, for their precious love, prayers, and essential encouragement towards this special project.

Thank you to my parents, Robert and Carol Upham for their love, support for higher education, family trips to the lake, and sense of humor, which made all the difference growmg up.

Thank you to my loving grandparents, Charles and Martha Upham, and Carlton and Tillie Thiel, who taught me to set goals, live life with a spirit of adventure, and to help others.

A sincere thank you to William and Helen Bille for their love, kindness and hospitality over the years.

My special thanks to Maryanne Haselow-Dulin of Editing Services for her expertise in layout and editing skills, and for providing valuable information to get this book to print.

Special appreciation to Camarie E. Bille for the author's photograph, hair design, and make-up artistry. Thank you to her photographer's assistant, Kensey Bille.

And to my brother Michael Upham in Keaau, Hawaii, a special thank you for contributing to the design concept of this book.

Contents

Contents

Introduction

Most busy parents of children birth to twelve years of age have limited time and many questions. The main purpose of this book is to give a considerable amount of important child-development information in an easy-to-read format. It would take years of academic study and parenting to gain the knowledge contained within these pages. The author wanted this parent reference book to include a wide variety of topics that are of concern to parents with children birth to twelve years of age.

Year after year, this essential information will help you gain the confidence you need to know what is expected at each stage of development.

This book is divided into five parts:
1. Newborn to thirty-six months
2. Three years to twelve years
3. Preschool topics of interest
4. School-age topics of interest
5. And more ... Special areas of interest

This valuable parenting tool will help you better understand your child at each age level and help your child reach his or her maximum potential.

Newborn to Thirty-Six Months

- Sensory Awareness

- Communication/Learning

Newborn to Thirty-Six Months

Looking into the eyes of your precious newborn brings powerful feelings of joy and responsibility. When his or her tiny eyes try to focus on your face, an overwhelming sense of love and exhilaration fills your heart. This new life is looking to you to feed, clothe, hold, talk, teach, and love him or her.

Ifyou already have children, they will need time to adjust to the newest family member. The family dynamics will change somewhat, so you will need to reassure the older siblings that they are important and loved, too.

Explain to your other children that babies need a lot of care and attention. Allow the older children to be helpers (in small ways) by getting a diaper, showing toys, talking to the baby, and so forth, to develop a bond between the children.

During the first part of this book, you will be taken down the developmental journey of newborn to thirty-six months. Your child will change from a completely dependent infant to a walking, talking, finger-feeding toddler.

Most parents have many questions in the early stages of parenthood. Itis hoped that in the following pages, you will find the answers to the important ones.

Newborn

Sensory Awareness

- Attends briefly to movement and objects.
- Attends to sounds and voices.
- Visually moves eyes to the middle to look at faces and objects.
- Is more attentive when in an upright position.
- Can gaze at an object at 180° with uneven movements.
- Has a rooting mouth reflex.
- Demonstrates a primitive hand-grasp reflex.
- Attends to straight, angled, black/white and striped designs.

Communication/Learning

- Attends to the parents'/people's faces.
- Cries when hungry.
- Cries when wet.
- Cries when startled.
- Quiets when picked up and swaddled.

One Month

Sensory Awareness

- Shows startle reflex to louder noises.
- Eyes work together with better focus.
- Attempts to turn head towards sounds.
- Sucks hand when on the tummy (prone) position.
- Begins to suck and look at hands.
- Moves body or quiets to a soft rattle.
- Becomes quiet when hearing a familiar voice.

Infants require lots of love and a gentle touch to grow and thrive.

Infants need adults to talk to them daily in order to start the language interaction foundation.

Communication/Learning

- Looks at a face briefly.
- Usually stops crying when held.
- Becomes quiet when hearing a familiar voice.
- Produces *e* and *a* vowel sounds.
- Cries when hungry.
- Cries when wet or uncomfortable.

Two Months

Sensory Awareness

- Begins to watch hands at the end of the 2nd month.
- Starts to mouth objects.
- Head and eye movements are not yet separate.
- Eyes are focusing more smoothly on faces and things.
- Keeps gaze on an object until it is out of sight.
- Uses slow-changing glances between two different toys.
- Starts to repeat his or her own movements.

Communication/Learning

- Smiles when talked to by adults and children.
- Looks at the face of the person who is speaking.
- Begins to squeal, coo, and laugh.
- Produces sucking noises.
- Expresses single vowels *(ah, eh, uh)*.
- Responds to her own voice.
- Sometimes repeats the same vowel when cooing.
- Often cries when the parents leave the room.

Three Months

Sensory Awareness

- Looks in the direction of sounds and voices.
- Eyes follow brightly colored objects or clothing.
- Reaches out to grasp close objects.
- Likes to watch, touch, and mouth hands.
- Responds differently to clothing, toys, furniture, or bedding with varying textures.

Communication/Learning

- Will cry when hearing loud or angry-sounding vocal tones.
- Prefers pleasant vocal tones and will coo.
- Smiles sometimes when smiled at by others.
- Is becoming more aware of home environment.
- Laughs out loud when happy.
- Begins to produce two vowel syllables *(ah, ah,* or *eh, eh,* or *uh, uh).*
- Starts to look at the eyes of the person speaking.
- Smiles more at mother or caregiver than at others.

Four Months

Sensory Awareness

- Looks at toys or other objects and reaches towards them.
- Reaches for family members or caregivers.
- Mouths toys for oral (mouth) stimulation and exploration.
- Begins to search with eyes for toys that have fallen out of sight.

Communication/Learning

- Laughs aloud in verbal play.
- Coos, cries, and gurgles to people and toys.
- Turns head purposefully towards sounds and voices.
- Searches for the speaker.
- Acts frightened at loud voices.
- Vocalizes independently in sound play.
- Begins to produce p, b, m consonants.
- Moves and sometimes smiles to peek-a-boo.
- Begins to reach towards toys that have fallen out of view.

Five Months

Sensory Awareness

- Continues to mouth, shake, and bang toys and objects.
- Turns head to look for lost toys, spoons, and things.
- Looks back and forth between two objects.
- Grasps nearby objects and toys.
- Pats bottle or breast during feedings.
- Explores things with eyes and touch.

Communication/Play

- Smiles automatically at people.
- Tries to imitate smiles, frowns, and surprised looks.
- Can recognize parents, caregivers, and close relatives.
- Begins to recognize his or her own name when it is spoken.
- Produces *b, m, n, ah, ee, oo* sounds.
- Makes sounds to keep busy and happy.
- Plays peek-a-boo with parent.
- Appears to know words such as "bye bye," "daddy," and "mama."
- Can hold one or two objects when placed in hands.
- Gazes and reaches for a partially covered toy.
- Stares at unknown people.

Six Months

Sensory Awareness

- Increasingly explores toys and objects with all the senses: sight, hearing, smell, taste, and touch.
- Visually follows toys that drop to the floor.
- Looks to see if a toy or object will return after it falls.
- Touches and plays with feet.
- Listens to and can tell the difference between friendly and angry talking.

Communication/Learning

- Turns eyes towards sounds and voices.
- Produces several syllables.
- Appears to recognize immediate family members' names.
- Seems to enjoy music and singing.
- Vocalizes at a mirror.
- Vocalizes to toys.
- Smiles and shows excitement to feeding.
- Laughs, coos, gurgles, and cries to express happiness and unhappiness.
- Bangs toys on a plastic tray or floor.
- Cries when toys fall or are taken away.
- Can babble several sounds at a time.
- May produce the following sounds:/, *th, s, sh, z, m, n, b, d, u, e, ee, oh, ah,* and *oo.*

Seven Months

Sensory Awareness

- Appears to listen to most of the conversation between adults.
- May stop an activity when his or her name is called.
- Moves hands for pat-a-cake.
- Looks for objects dropped out of view.
- Gives visual attention to hands while playing or holding toys or objects.
- Recognizes familiar voices.

Communication/Learning

- Produces syllables such as *ba, da,* and *ka.*
- Seems to recognize the names of some common objects relating to care (bottle, bed, bathtub, diaper, blanket, car, house, etc.), when spoken.
- Begins babbling with voice inflection.
- Also vocalizes to a familiar children's song.
- Continues to interact with pat-a-cake and peek-a-boo.
- Matches body movements to gestures that are familiar.
- Finger-feeds small pieces of food such as cereal.
- Recognizes familiar faces.
- Tries to squeeze and stretch toys.

Eight Months

Sensory Awareness

- Will attempt to initiate new body movement seen in others.
- Starts to drop, throw, and watch toys after looking at them.
- Imitates clapping of hands during pat-a-cake.

Communication/Learning

- Will respond to name by eye contact, head-turning, and smiles.
- Says *dada, baba.*
- Imitates mouth movements.
- Reaches for toys that are farther away.
- Begins to push toys and objects.
- Repeats actions that cause noise in toys.
- Voice changes pitch up and down, like asking a question.
- Babbles longer sequences of nonwords like a sentence.
- Can imitate *ba, da, ka,* and tongue   clicks.
- Shakes head "no" at times.

Nine Months

Senson1 Awareness

- Reaches for objects and toys in a container.
- Smiles and pats at a mirror.
- Inspects toys and objects with hands and mouth.
- Starts to use crawling/locomotion to get objects and toys.
- Has increased visual awareness to size and texture of objects.
- Searches for an object under a sheer blanket.

Communication/Learning

- Waves *bye bye,* claps at pat-a-cake.
- Stops an activity when told "no-no."
- Tries to mimic sounds of adults.
- More consonants are appearing in babbling.
- Vocalizes loudly to get attention.
- Very little or no drooling.
- Recognizes mother and father.
- Listens to others while adults and children are speaking.
- Says "oh oh" when happy or excited.
- Can listen to speech for short periods and not be distracted by background noise.
- Animal noises such as dogs, cats, and birds startle or delight a child this age.
- Likes cause-and-effect toys that have music or voices.
- Moves objects and can turn one right side up when it is upside down.

Ten Months

Senso!}' Awareness

- Responds to music with body movements.
- Looks around a comer for toys and objects.
- Points, pokes, and touches with index finger.
- Begins to pull toys with a string attached.
- Starts to investigate busy box toys (pushing a squeak button, stroking a colored ball, or putting an index finger in a toy phone dial wheel).

Communication/Learning

- Uses the words "dada" and "mama" for parents.
- During play, is exploring spatial concepts (in/out, on/off, and up/down).
- Vocalizes jargon speech (sounds like a strange language) with normal sentence inflection.
- Sometimes tries to imitate simple one-syllable words.
- Follows simple one-step directions ("Where is the ball?" "Put that down.""Come here, please." "Wave bye bye.""Say mama.' " "No, no. Don't touch that.").

Eleven Months

Senson1 Awareness

- Listens to speech for longer periods.
- Watches and tries to operate a simple cause-and-effect toy.
- Stirs fingers in a cup.
- Looks at pictures in a toddler board book, which usually has very simple pictures or one picture per page.

Communication/Learning

- Babbles longer sentence-like utterances; may have some words.
- Will say three or more words on a regular basis.
- Can drop toys in and out of a box, plastic block container, etc.
- Can hold a sippy cup with handles or a narrow sippy cup to drink.
- Understands simple requests.

Twelve and Thirteen Months

Sensory Awareness

- Looks in certain directions for objects when directed by adults.
- Has more coordinated oral/motor movements of the mouth.
- Likes to tear and crinkle paper.
- Eye-hand coordination is starting to develop for such activities as putting a large wooden peg in a Peg-Board.
- Tries to turn the page of a toddler board book.

Communication/Learning

- Takes the cover off a small box.
- Shows different emotions through facial/body expressions and vocalizations.
- Points to toys, people, animals, and objects.
- Loves cause-and-effect toys.
- Is able to give a toy or object to a parent or caregiver.
- Will point and use jargon speech to get toys and objects.
- Puts hands over face and laughs during peek-a-boo.
- Understands simple needs questions by facial expressions, words, and gestures.
- Pushes an arm through a sleeve when assisted by adults.
- Tries to push buttons on household furniture and appliances.

> Always know your child's whereabouts at this age.

Fourteen to Seventeen Months

Sensory Awareness

- Searches for toys under a blanket or box that is not transparent.
- Looks at picture books and can turn pages (board books still are the best to reduce tom pages).
- Can stack up to three wooden or plastic blocks vertically.
- Can begin to make a crayon mark on paper when shown how to by an adult.
- Begins to point to a few simple pictures in a book (e.g., ball, mommy, bottle, etc.).
- Follows a few one-step directions for identifying facial and body parts ("Point to your eyes.""Where is your mouth?").

Communication/Learning

- Speaks up to twelve words.
- Communicates by single words and facial expressions or hand gestures.
- Will begin to put two words together sometimes.
- Points and shows objects to adults.
- Labels simple objects around the house.
- Vocabulary continues to expand during this stage.
- Frequently used sounds are *w, t, d, h, n, b, p,* and *h.*

Eighteen to
Twenty-One Months

Senson1 Awareness

- Enjoys listening to stories and looking at picture books.
- Likes to listen to children's songs and nursery rhymes.
- Begins to ask for food when hungry and water or milk when thirsty.
- Moves body, swings (in a child safety swing), and tries to dance to music.

Communication/Language

- Uses two- orthree-word sentences.
- Can say his or her name when referring to self.
- Begins to use pronouns ("I," "me," and "you").
- Will imitate one- and two-syllable simple words.
- Points to a few body parts.
- By twenty-one months, can point to pictures of clothing and identify shoes, socks, pants, diaper, or top with some consistency.
- Comprehends simple two-word commands.

Twenty-Two to Twenty-Seven Months

Communication and Comprehension

- Can understand the concept of "another."
- Responds to the directions "in" and "on."
- Begins to follow two-step directions.
- Is able to understand "yes/no" questions.
- Points to five or more picture cards or pictures in a book.
- Understands family names/categories (baby, mama, daddy, grandma, papa, sister, brother, etc.).
- Can identify one of something (toys, foods, objects).
- Listens longer to simple storybooks.
- Is beginning to understand "small" and "big."
- Is able to visually identify household and daily care objects by use.
- Remembers where favorite toys are kept.
- Can explore a mechanical toy before being shown how to operate it.

Expression

- Is starting to use his or her name more.
- Can imitate first and last name.
- Names familiar objects in the environment (home, store, relatives' homes, daycare, etc.).
- Imitates parts of children's songs and rhymes.

By twenty-seven months, a child has at
least a 300-word vocabulary. Very
verbal children may have a larger
vocabulary.

Learning

- Selects own toys from others.
- Begins to draw up-and-down and side-to-side strokes with a crayon.
- Holds crayons with fingers, though still a little uncoordinated.
- Tries to make circles with crayons.
- Likes to build four- to six-cubed towers.
- Begins to unscrew a jar lid that is not on very tight.
- Can hold, try to kick, throw, and carry a ball.
- Begins simple problem-solving strategies.

Twenty-Eight to Thirty Months

Communication and Comprehension

- Word association through use is expanding ("What do you eat?" "What do you put on your feet?" etc.).
- Understands more names and pictures of functional objects.
- Comprehends 300 to 1,000 words.
- Is becoming aware of simple opposites *(in/out, on/off, up/down, big/little, hot/cold,* etc.).
- Can begin to match identical toys and common objects.

Expression

- Repeats two or more numbers correctly.
- Uses the *I* pronoun sometimes to refer to self.
- Names one or more colors correctly.
- Repeats what adults and other children say.
- Asks "what" questions about objects and pictures.
- Asks names of simple activities.
- Points to and repeats at least six body parts.
- Asks the location of certain people, animals, toys, food, and objects.
- Uses plurals (adding *s* to some words).

Learning

- Plays near children but not usually with them.
- Builds taller block towers (6-8 cubes).

- Is able to sit a little longer to do four- to six-piece puzzles (fruit, shapes, animals).
- Likes soft stuffed animals to hug and talk to during play.
- Likes to push buttons on musical, lighted, and talking toys.
- Prefers simple animal and shorter cartoon musical videos.
- Enjoys hitting bongos, ringing bells, and shaking musical toys.
- Is starting to be interested in Play Dough®; may try to put in his or her mouth.

> A recipe for homemade play dough with flour, water, and salt made without food coloring may be more appropriate at this stage.

- Small tents and playhouses provide favorite activities.

> Smaller outside play equipment needs adult supervision at all times.

Thirty-One Months to Thirty-Six Months

Communication and Comprehension

- Understands the meaning for simple verbs (action words).
- Is beginning to know common adjectives or describing words for color, size, shape, and texture, etc.).
- Can match a block or object of the same color.
- Understands spatial concepts *(under, on, front, behind, in, out)*.
- Seems to know quantity concepts *(one, two, many)* and responds to requests such as "Show me ..." one (or two) of something.
- Understands longer sentences.
- Shows an interest in how objects work.

Expression

- Knows his or her gender.
- Is able to say first and last names.
- Tells of something that happened recently.
- Uses action words when looking at pictures in a book.
- Repeats two or three numbers.
- Counts to three.
- Produces 50o/o--75% of consonants.
- Uses more pronouns *(I, he, she, me, him,* and *her)*.
- Has a vocabulary of 500-1,000 words.

Learning

- Can follow simple two-step directions with visual cues.
- Enjoys counting toys or objects (one to three).
- Copies a circle drawn by an adult.
- Is beginning to cut with simple child's scissors.
- Loves to look at photographs of self and family members.
- Likes finger painting.

> Wearing an old shirt or covering will protect the child's clothing.

- Still plays near other children but is beginning to join in group activities.
- Enjoys building wooden roads to roll trains and cars on.
- Enjoys singing along with familiar songs and using simple hand, arm, and body gestures.
- Is getting more coordinated; can put together big-piece puzzles.

Three Years to Twelve Years

- Articulation/Speech

- Language

- Play/Leaming

- Social/Emotional

- Self-Help Skills

Three Years to Twelve Years

The developmental stages from three years to twelve years covers a great deal of information.

You may choose to focus on the portions that relate to the current age or ages of your children. This part of the book can be revisited year after year as your child moves to the next level of development.

Many useful points are introduced to help you better understand articulation/speech development, language expansion, play/learning references, social/emotional changes, and self-help skills for each unique year.

The information received for each developmental year will give valuable insight for helping your child learn.

Some of the reading and writing skills can be practiced during weekends and summer vacations. Learning stores are excellent places to buy materials to expand math, spelling, reading, grammar, and writing skills. Remember that teachers are only part of the learning equation. Parental involvement is essential for a child to be a successful student.

When parents demonstrate a positive attitude towards reading or learning, their children will follow their example.

The Three-Year-Old

Speech/Articulation

- Three-and-a-half-year-olds can pronounce *m, n, ng, p,* *f h,* and *w.*

Language

- More words are used to express ideas and concepts.
- Sentence length is three or more words.
- "What" and "why" questions are expressed.
- Nouns and verbs are used in simple phrases.
- Listening skills increase for names of objects, people, and places.
- New vocabulary is used to express simple needs and things around the home.
- Communication frustration lessens as vocabulary expands.

Play/Learning

- Motor development increases; three-year-olds enjoy ball play, scooter boards, tricycles, running, dancing and waffling their arms and legs.
- Musical toys and toys that talk are popular.
- Counting to five is fun.
- Swings with safety seats and small plastic slides, when used with adult supervision, are appropriate.
- Sandboxes with toys and plastic pails/shovels delight them.
- Play Dough® keeps them busy.

Social/Emotional

- Is more interactive with peers and adults.
- Has fewer and shorter tantrums.
- Likes to please parents, caregivers, and preschool teachers.
- The personality and mood development is almost complete.

Self-Help Skills

- Tries to feed himself with a spoon.
- Drinks well from a sippy cup.
- May be able to manage a small amount of liquid in a cup with two handles.
- Still enjoys finger foods.

> Cut foods into small pieces to avoid choking, especially such foods as grapes and hot dogs, which are higher risk for choking.

- Tries to put on shirt and slacks, but parents still need to help with dressing.

The Four-Year-Old

Seech/Articulation

- The four-year-old can pronounce *k, b, d, g,* and *r.*

> Stuttering or dysfluency can be observed in young children as phrases get longer and stress to speak sometimes increases.
> Give your child plenty of time to express thoughts and needs.

Language

- Pronouns begin to surface in conversational speech.
- Sentence length is four or more words.
- Articles and connecting words appear *(and, or, a, as, the)*.
- Memory skills for past and present experiences are evident.
- Vocabulary continues to grow for nouns, verbs, and simple adjectives.

Play/Learning

- Puzzles with various shapes, colors, and sizes
- Kitchen sets with artificial food and utensils
- Blocks, Leggos® for building things
- Toy trucks, airplanes, and action figures
- Sand and water play
- Blowing bubbles
- Finger painting, pasting paper and textured objects together (sensory art activities)

- Stuffed animals provide fun, comfort, and play opportunities.
- Dolls with furniture, clothes, and utensils are fun for girls and boys.

Social/Emotional

- More group play and cooperation between peers is developing.
- Has fears about being separated from parent at stores or anywhere with lots of room and people.
- Experiences night dreams that can be frightening.
- Needs a great deal of positive self-esteem building at this age.

Self-Help Skills

- Wants to do more things for daily care.
- Drinking from a cup is improving.
- Begins to brush teeth independently.
- Can follow simple one-step directions.
- Eats with little assistance (except for cutting food into small pieces).
- Needs help with buttons, snaps, and zippers.

The Five-Year-Old

Seech/Articulation

- The five-year-old can pronounce *sh, s,* and *ch.*

Language

- Enjoys retelling stories read to her.
- Vocabulary rapidly advances because the child usually starts school at this age.
- Inspects objects to see how they function.
- Is very curious about size, shape, colors, and textures of objects.
- Learns more spatial concepts and is able to follow directions better.
- Reverses the pronouns "I/me" sometimes.
- Simple sentence structures are expanding.
- Likes to ask lots of "what," "who," and "why" questions.

Play/Learning

- Organized group activities hold a five-year-old's attention.
- Eye-hand movements become more coordinated, and printing alphabet letters, coloring, and painting skills improves.

Parents and teachers need to keep imaginary stories simple because children at this <u>age</u> are concrete thinkers.

Labeling simple objects around the house with printed index cards will help build visual sight-word recognition.

To teach categories (groups) of animals, people, furniture, jewelry, vehicles, buildings, insects, food, sports, places, and toys, use basic phonics cards or alphabet cards with a single picture and printed word. You can make your own cards by cutting out magazine pictures, gluing them to index cards, and printing the word below the picture.

Social/Emotional

- Enjoys visiting stores, zoos, discovery museums, school, friends' homes, etc.
- Siblings and friends are important to the five-year-old.
- Loves to spend special time alone with a parent.
- Tries to impress friends with facial expressions, toys, and motor skills.

Self-Help Skills

- Can perform simple daily grooming tasks with adult assistance.
- Puts toys away in a box, on a shelf, or in a closet when requested by parents.

- Enjoys selecting clothes to wear, even though the selections don't always match.
- Have favorite clothes and shoes that they prefer to wear over and over.

> It's important to check the style, color, or texture that appeals to your five-year-old. When you shop, take him with you.

The Six-Year-Old

Seech/Articulation

- The six-year-old can pronounce *t,* v, *l,* and *th.*

Language

- Has a vocabulary of at least 10,000 words.
- Has a short attention span for activities.
- May need picture reminders and word charts for routines and chores.
- Begins to express more thoughts, feelings, and needs.

> Parents need to keep directions short and to the point for the six-year-old.

- Now begins to learn color words, animal words, and categories.
- Recognizes alphabet letters and simple words.
- Learns short vowel words, rhyming, consonant blend words and meanings.
- Writes short sentences starting with the word "the."
- Matches pictures and simple sentences.
- Listens to sentences and responds with "yes/no."
- Can complete simple spelling tasks of three and four letter words.
- Begins to create some plural words using *s* and *ies.*

> The six-year-old needs a lot of phonics reading and writing tasks to support word practice. Vowel review activities also are beneficial.

Play/Learning

- May reverse numbers and letters when writing.
- Computes simple addition problems; object counters and visual examples are excellent in building this skill.
- Likes the alphabet song.

> Reading, phonics, and new sight words are the foundation for developing reading skills at this age.

- Continues to develop fine motor skills; puzzles, stringing wooden beads, lacing cards, cause-and-effect toys, and scissor activities all enhance coordination.
- Increases gross motor abilities for throwing and kicking balls, climbing, skipping, jumping, and hopping.
- Still has some difficulty with eye-hand coordination.
- Starts to know the right foot from the left foot.

> Beginning phonics cards and tapes help promote reading skills.

Social/Emotional

- Likes to act like a ham, but can be shy at times.
- Has difficulty in making choices of toys, activities, clothes, food, etc.
- Shows opposite behaviors and words to express thoughts/ideas/ opinions.
- May be stubborn to parents' rules.

- Wants to be close to parents emotionally but independent at the same time.
- Friends and teachers are important; tends to act her best for teachers.

Self-Help Skills

- Bowel and bladder accidents happen when play is intense and he forgets to go to the bathroom.
- Can be a fussy eater with definite favorite foods and textures.
- Sometimes is slow getting dressed.

The Seven-Year-Old

Seech/Articulation

- The seven-year-old can pronounce a *z* and *zh*.

Language

- Vocabulary takes a surge due interest and practice in reading.
- Begins reciting the four seasons and months of the year.
- Knows simple categories of foods, furniture, people, toys, buildings, sports, and animals.
- Tries to imitate friends' talk and mannerisms.
- Completes sentences with one-word responses.
- Writes simple nouns, beginning verbs, rhyming words, and color words in sentences.
- Adds suffixes *s, ing,* and *ed* to words.
- Is learning and writing sentences with question marks.
- Is introduced to words in the dictionary.
- Can complete basic crossword puzzles.
- Uses adjectives for size, shape, and colors.
- Understands homonyms (dear/deer, ant/aunt).

> Taking your child on trips to the
> local library promotes literacy.

Play/Learning

- May need to wear glasses for reading; will get a vision and hearing screening when entering school.
- Coordination for using playground equipment mcreases.
- Phonics is beginning to make sense, so reading is becoming more fun.
- Is beginning to sit with books, trying to read the easier picture books.
- Sports are becoming more interesting.
- Will participate in art projects that require glitter, glue, washable markers, gel pens, and stickers.

Social/Emotional

- Needs to be taught respect for other people's property (toys, school supplies, clothing, etc.).
- Has a lot of energy, but is becoming more herself; appears calmer to family members.
- Is very sensitive to constructive pointers; believes others are pointing out weaknesses.
- Is concerned that parents and teachers approve of him.
- Expresses more about feelings and things of which she is afraid.

> Parents require extra patience to listen to the big/little problems their seven-year-olds perceive about themselves.

Self-Help Skills

- Has become mainly independent in most grooming and dressing tasks.
- May still need adult assistance for rinsing after a shampoo.
- Can now help fold towels, bring small wastebaskets to be emptied, and make his own bed.

The Eight-Year-Old

Speech/Articulation

- Most speech sounds should be developed by now.

> Speech pathologists will still see some
> children for frontal and side (lateral) lisps,
> in which the sounds of *s, sh,* and *ch* are
> distorted.
> Other sounds that give some children
> difficulty are *r, l;* substitutions of *w/r, o/r*
> and *wll* may be observed.

Language

- Vocabulary expands to 18,000 words.
- Listening to parents and teachers really advances this year.
- Social language or pragmatic skills also improve (initiating, continuing and ending conversations; turn taking; listening; reading facial expressions and body language).
- Reads sentences and writes "yes/no" responses.
- Composes three-word verb phrase completion tasks in writing exercises.
- Capitalization for beginning sentences is reviewed.
- Is taught proper nouns (people, places, holidays, days, and months of the year).
- Is introduced to beginning punctuation in simple sentences.

- Identifies declarative sentences (making a statement), interrogative sentences (asking a question), and exclamatory sentences (showing excitement or surprise).
- Learns simple contractions.
- Uses singular plurals in writing exercises.
- Opposite words are explained.
- Learns more homonyms (words that sound the same but have different meanings).
- Practices synonyms (similar meanings/different words).
- Learns to address envelopes.
- Now can correctly sequence a five-part sentence.
- Uses "two," "too," and "to" correctly in   sentences.
- Uses "a," "and," and "an" phrases.
- Develops beginning dictionary skills.
- Expands verb use and knowledge.
- Learns the past-tense words "was," "were," "thrown," "seen," and "became."

Social/Emotional

- Becomes more outgoing and friendly this year.
- Better communication skills make meeting new friends easier.
- Self-esteem is peaking with new confidence.
- Teasing from peers and siblings still go   hand-in-hand.
- Sometimes feels left out when younger siblings require a lot of his parents' attention.

> This is a year to spend special one-on-one time with your child, talking and building memories.

Self-Help Skills

- Can follow at least two-step directions when jobs are presented.
- With parental supervision, enjoys simple mixing of cookies, muffins, and pudding.

> Parents can begin to assign a few chores/jobs to build self-discipline and self-esteem in the eight-year-old, such as:
> - Folding towels and wash cloths
> - Sweeping the floor
> - Dusting low surfaces that have been cleared of glass objects
> - Feeding a pet **dry** food in a bowl
> - Picking up toys
> - Putting dirty clothes in a hamper

The Nine-Year-Old

S eeech/Articulation

- Is correctly producing most or all speech sounds.

> Ifa lisp for *s, z,* and *s* blend words is still present, and an overbite or under bite is still evident, parents should consult a dentist.

> Sometimes children will substitute *o/r* and *w/r* in words. This substitution can be due to an auditory awareness-processing deficit. Auditory training devices with earphones can be useful for some students to focus on articulation.

Language

- Vocabulary expansion doubles between eight years and ten years.
- Spatial concept knowledge is established.
- Following directions becomes easier.
- Can accomplish more writing tasks of *s, ed,* and *ing* endings to words.
- Definitions/meanings of science and social studies start to make more sense.
- Works on alphabetizing words.
- Takes on more dictionary practice for definitions, entry words, and guidewords.
- Practices journal writing.

- Is reading paragraphs and answering "wh" questions.
- Works at subject-predicate tasks.
- Completes rhyming word identification exercises.
- Uses proper nouns and compound nouns correctly.
- Writes thank-you notes.
- Understands topic sentence development.
- Uses words "like" and "as" to compare objects, people, places, and things.
- Has more pronoun practice in sentences, both verbal and written.
- Enjoys reading and discussing legends and fictional tales.
- Is introduced to colons and hyphens.

Play/Learning

- Likes competitions in sports, jobs, and schoolwork.
- Time is understood and enjoys wearing a watch to time himself.
- May develop her own timetable to complete jobs and activities.

> This age would be a good time to introduce an alarm clock.

- Riding bikes, skateboards, and Rollerblades, and going swimming are popular.

> Use appropriate safety helmets and padding to avoid injuries.

- Flashcards are appropriate to strengthen multiplication and division skills.
- Division problems are becoming more complex.
- Small computer math toys also can promote math skills.

Social/Emotional

- May experience stressful or negative nighttime dreams.
- Sons tend to want more one-on-one time with Dad or another male.
- Needs to adjust to having several teachers throughout the school day.
- Enjoys going to friends' and grandparents' homes.
- Becomes more critical of himself than others around him.
- Exhibits kinder behavior to siblings.

Self-Help Skills

- May start asking for a pet of her own to love.
- Enjoys organizing collections neatly on shelves.
- Becomes more independent with daily grooming and chores.
- Responds well to positive praise for keeping rooms clean and putting clothes in the hamper.

> Since children this age enjoy going shopping, make a list and let them help find the items in the store.

The Ten-Year-Old

Speech/Articulation

- Will have mastered most articulation sounds.

> Some children may still have lisps due to dental problems.
> Other children demonstrate weak tongue muscles or an uncoordinated tongue, possibly due to neurological reasons.
> Other children's poor auditory listening skills hinder making corrections.
> Still others may have given up and don't want to make the effort to change their speech.

> Practicing at home with articulation worksheets and working with the speech pathologist will help your child overcome ongoing articulation problems.

Lane

- Vocabulary development can reach 40,000 words. While they may know this number of words, they won't always use them in conversational speech.
- Continues to improve alphabetizing skills.
- Learns about a book's table of contents, the index, and note taking.
- Practices compound words.
- Can identify a paragraph's main points during listening activities.

- Learns to develop a business letter.
- Can write a party invitation.
- Uses apostrophes in sentences.
- Can write a story with characters, setting, plot, and ending.
- Develops an outline.
- Idioms start to make more sense now.

Play/Learning

- Art activities interest both boys and girls Gewelry, model cars and airplanes, gel pens, miniature wooden furniture, latch hooking, painting pictures, sewing with needles and thread, etc.).
- Watches are becoming more important.
- Girls may enjoy the historical dolls, clothes, furniture, accessories, and books that go along with them (e.g., the American Girls® series), which promote literacy and provide childhood memories.
- Collections of all sorts are popular.
- Motor skills for sports, dance, and gymnastics mcrease.
- Computer games of all kinds fascinate this age level.
- Will be learning fractions in school.
- Teachers expect more homework.
- Memory skills for grammar rules and organizing paragraphs advance.
- Music lessons for a variety of instruments can be introduced.

> "Series" books are appropriate for the ten-year-old. Check with your local bookstores and libraries; they can be very helpful in selecting reading material.

> A significant leap in expectations for
> learning occurs for the ten-year-old.

Social/Emotional

- Exhibits politeness and kindness to other people.
- Respect for parents and teachers peaks this year.
- Sleepovers with friends become popular.
- Hormones and emotional status appear to be more even.

> This is the perfect age to build lots of
> family memories, since ten-year-olds really
> like family togetherness.

Self-Help Skills

- Messy rooms are common; children need positive rewards and consistent expectations to build good habits.
- Appetites are growing along with the child.
- Children appear to have strong candy cravings, but providing healthy options or smaller fun-size candy bars can ward off the craving for sweets.
- Supply healthy snack foods such as yogurt, fruit, cheese, milk, nuts, carrots, peanut butter, and whole-grain crackers.

> Ten-year-olds yearn to earn more spending money. Be
> creative to help them add to their earning potential.

The Eleven-Year-Old

Speech/Articulation

- The rate of speech speeds up because this age group has a lot to talk about.

> The average child this age exhibits normal articulation. However, for those children still having a few problems, having them practice reading aloud with a tape recorder can help with self-monitoring. The auditory listening device and headphone system sold at places such as Radio Shack will also help auditory listening skills. Again, you can check with your dentist to see if the tooth and bite alignment may be contributing to the situation.

Language

- Social language skills are still developing.
- Taking turns and appropriate loudness levels still need some fine-tuning.
- Humor and laughter are a significant part of the language experienced with peers.
- Becomes quite talented in expressing to adults what she needs and thinks.

> Early adolescence can bring
> disagreements that pop up on a variety of
> issues. Parents need to remain calm and
> firm, and to develop a new dimension of
> patience.

- Uses the demonstratives "this," "that," "these," and "those" in speech and writing.
- Uses more intense adjectives as his moods rise and fall.
- Comprehends the use of opposites and synonyms.
- Expresses more complex definitions for vocabulary.
- Reviews alphabetizing, table of contents, and index.
- Explores the various sections of the newspaper for information expansion.
- Makes sentence fragments into full sentences in writing tasks.
- Participates in more letter writing tasks.
- Develops more complex paragraphing in writing exercises.
- Begins proofreading writing activities.
- Uses adverbs that tell "how," "when," and "where" more frequently.
- Is introduced to and practices poetry writing.
- Reviews the articles "a," "am," and "the."

Play/Learning

- Ball kicking, throwing, and catching skills become more coordinated.
- Sports performance becomes more important to some children.

- Physical activities such as running, walking, biking, Rollerblading, gymnastics, exercise equipment (e.g., an indoor bike), roller-skating, basketball, soccer, volleyball, swimming, and ice skating help release boundless energy.
- Studies maps and graphs in more detail.
- Practices dictionary use for locating words, definitions, and pronunciations.
- Participates more in reading and discussing the main points of a story.
- Reads and writes featured newspaper editorial articles.
- Writes book reports on library books.

> More note-taking practice is essential to build strong skills for future grade levels.

Social/Emotional

- Has a strong need to be liked by friends.
- Wants to fit in and follow the fads of clothing, music, hairstyles, etc.

> It is important to know your child's friends and their parents.

- Begins to take an interest in sports figures and film stars.
- Is a little more self-absorbed in his looks and life.
- Questions the authority of parents, teachers, and other adults (needs limits set by adults).
- Needs to have worthy role models in order to develop respect for adults.

Self-Help Skills

- Seems to be eating nonstop; is entering a growth spurt.
- Jobs seem less important; making her bed and picking up dirty clothes is a daily bother.

> Parents need to be consistent in expecting responsibilities to be met. Self-discipline to carry out daily tasks builds character and self-respect for the child.

> More shopping trips will be required this year due to weight or height gains.

The Twelve-Year-Old

Articulation/Speech

- Fewer children are in speech therapy for articulation errors.
- The *s* and *r* consonants may still be a concern for some children.

> By this age, most children have worked with dedication to change their speech with the professional expertise of the speech language pathologist. A few are losing motivation and sometimes ask for a break from speech therapy.
>
> As they mature, some return to speech therapy when they realize their speech deficit could decrease job opportunities or negatively affect relations with peers.

Language

- Expresses longer syllable words through conversation and writing.
- Thinks about world events and expresses ideas/opinions.
- Has developed her written language and grammar skills well.
- Reviews the four types of sentences: declarative, interrogative, imperative, and exclamatory.
- Language processing and comprehension skills surge this year.
- Performs more punctuation practice in language class.

- Reviews common and proper nouns.
- Uses transitive and intransitive verbs in writing tasks.
- Also reviews direct and indirect objects this year.
- Reviews auxiliaries (helping verbs).
- Writes letters to friends and relatives.
- Diagrams sentences.
- Reviews adverbs in sentence practice.
- Reviews subject-verb agreement in writing exercises.
- Practices using quotation marks in sentences and paragraphs.
- Expands on advanced dictionary tasks.

Play/Learning

- More coordination in hands and feet; balance is improved.
- Interest in physical activity and sports increases.
- Youth groups for music, sports, art, crafts, taking care of animals, etc., build character and cooperation.
- Develops new test-taking skills.
- Develops advanced report-writing skills.
- Enhances study skills for curriculum subjects.

Social/Emotional

- Enjoys talking on the phone to friends and relatives.
- Mood swings due to changing hormones are still evident, but evening out.
- Boys and girls begin to take notice of each other in a more positive manner.

- Girls begin a fast physical growth spurt. Weight evens out or is sometimes lost when height is added.
- Some girls begin menstruation.
- Parents note fewer disagreements.
- Some verbal differences with siblings can still be heard.

> Continue to talk to your preteen about school, friends, or anything he wants to share.
> Keep rules for curfews.
> Know where your preteen is going and get to know her friends.

Self-Hel Skills

- Depending on how trustworthy a preteen is, a mature twelve-year-old can be at home alone for short periods of time.
- Enjoys eating and needs more calories when active in sports.

> Before leaving mature twelve-year-olds at home for short periods of time, go over safety and house rules. Ifyou're not at ease leaving your twelve-year-old at home, then wait until you are comfortable.

> Continue to promote daily jobs and expand expectations as your child can handle them.

Preschool Topics of Interest

- Tips to Help Your Child Sleep

- Home Safety Suggestions for Young Children

- Tips on Buying the Right Toys

- Selecting a High-Standards Preschool

- Preschooler Separation Problems

Preschool Topics of Interest

This section discusses special topics related to the preschooler. Each segment provides practical tips and applications for the parents ofpreschoolers.

New parents often list lack of sleep as one adjustment problem to the new baby's coming home, so practical tips to help your child sleep better are given.

Now that a child is sharing your home, safety becomes even more important. Useful suggestions are presented to make your home safer and to reduce the risk of injury to your child.

The guide to buying the right toys provides important insights on child-play skills. Various types oftoys with respect to their value to learning are reviewed.

The segment "Selecting a High Standards Preschool" provides important information to help make the best decision for your child. These tips can increase your child's odds for a more fulfilling preschool experience.

Overcoming preschool separation problems examines solutions to make your mornings run smoother.

The preschool years give you the opportunity to experience your childhood memories all over again through your child's eyes. This stage is truly a fun, memorable, and special time in a parent's life.

Tips to Help Your Child Sleep

Babies

Sleep problems can be related to a variety of possibilities. Check with your pediatrician if this has been going on for a while.

Some possible related problems could be trapped gas, muscle pain, digestive disorders, and food or milk allergies.

Babies sleep more than toddlers. If babies are hungry or uncomfortable being wet, they will not sleep. Check to see if they are too cold or too hot.

Tips

- Check for a gas bubble.
- Feed if hungry.
- Change the diaper.
- Rock them back to sleep.

Toddlers and Preschool Children

For toddlers and school-age children, a nighttime routine is important.

TiQS

- Avoid giving your child foods and beverages with large amounts of sugar and caffeine, especially at bedtime. Be alert to food dyes, which can cause extra active behavior.

- Play a calming lullaby or nature sounds of the ocean, rain, birds, and so forth.
- Record your own voice reading storybooks or singing soft children's songs.
- A short loving conversation while being rocked in a dimly lit room works.
- A routine bedtime reading period can promote special memories, expand vocabulary, enhance literacy, and encourage sleep.
- A favorite blanket, nightlight, or stuffed animal can add to a sense of security and promote sleep.

Home Safety Suggestions
for Young Children

Tips

- Keep extra keys for interior doors in your home in case your child accidentally locks himself in a room.
- Keep doors that lead to the basement locked. Consider placing a lock higher on the door that cannot be opened by little fingers.
- Securely attach gates to walls by staircases.
- Install blinds and curtains on large glass doors and windows to lessen the chance of children walking into them.
- Install stops on windows.
- Place plastic covers over electric outlets.
- Read about houseplants and purchase only those that are safe around children.
- Check for lead-base paint in older buildings. Law requires special cleanup and disposal.
- Keep the water temperature under 120°F.
- Purchase a crib with safe measurements between slats (no wider than a soft drink can).

Tips on Buying the Right Toys

The following questions need to be considered when buying toys for your child:

- Is the toy age-appropriate for your child?
- Does the toy light up, play music, or have a voice/talking component?
- Is the toy well constructed, with no small pieces that could be swallowed by young children?
- Does the toy create imaginative play experiences?
- Can the toy be washed or cleaned?
- Are the action figures or dolls appropriate or do they promote violence?
- Does the toy require batteries? If so, an ample supply will be needed.
- Is the toy educational? Does it teach counting, the alphabet, or math, spelling, and vocabulary skills?
- Does the toy teach concepts such as shapes, colors, textures, and sizes?

Ti e

- Child tape recorders or child CD players are great for promoting music appreciation.

Selecting a
High-Standards Preschool

The following questions should be asked when looking for a high-standards preschool for your child:

- Are the staff cheerful, seem to enjoy working with small children, and do they demonstrate patience?
- Is there a routine or curriculum that is followed consistently?
- What types of skills will the preschool be teaching your child?
- What are the meals and snacks? Are they nutritious?
- Will you as a parent need to provide meals and snacks?
- What kinds of toys, books, computers, art, and music activities are offered? How often do the staff clean and sanitize their toys?
- Is the building large enough? How many children are in each room?
- Does the building have good ventilation, lighting, heat, and cooling systems?
- Are the building and outdoor areas gated and safe from busy roads or water?
- Is there enough safe playground equipment? Is it in good working order?

Tips

- The staff need to be properly trained in child development, CPR, and appropriate curriculum for preschool children.

- Check how the preschool has done in state inspections.
- Talk with other parents who currently send their children to the preschool you are considering.

Preschooler Separation Problems

Transitioning from home to a preschool or day care provider can be difficult for some children. The following tips may help make the transition more comfortable for you and your child.

Tips

- Try to give baths the night before and select clothes to save time in the morning.
- Give your child plenty of time to wake up and eat breakfast.
- To eliminate hunger tantrums, provide a small snack for children who eat breakfast outside the home.
- Sit for a short time to hug and show affection to reassure your child that you love him. Talk about how much fun he will have in preschool that day.
- Allow your child to bring a special toy, stuffed animal, or blanket in the car. Not all preschools will allow personal items due to potential outbreaks of lice.
- Clinging, crying behaviors usually decrease as the child adjusts to the new teacher/day care provider, peers, and surroundings.
- If your child does not adjust, observe her at the preschool or day care provider's home. If the match does not appear to have been a good one, try to find other arrangements.

School-Age Topics of Interest

- Teaching Direction-Following Concepts to Your Child

- Promoting Reading and Literacy Skills

- Enhancing Your Child's Gifts and Talents

- Helping Your Child Become a Better Student

School-Age Topics of Interest

The school years will require lots of time and patience. During the next thirteen years, your child's academic skills, character traits, talents, and respect for others will be molded.

Make the time to build positive family relationships. Experience a variety of family events, vacations, and moments. Take lots of photographs and video movies to help recall enjoyable childhood memories.

As a parent you will have a large role in contributing time and money to develop your child's interests. Investigate your child's strengths, talents, and interests, and look for ways to develop them.

Youth organizations, clubs, and religious youth groups can enrich your child's life. Children can learn respect, leadership traits, valuable social skills, and develop meaningful friendships through participating inthese activities.

Young people can have a positive influence in their own communities. They can pick up litter in parks, plant trees, volunteer at food pantries, and raise funds for worthy causes.

The elementary school years set the stage for the upcoming teen years. The attitudes and respect for values instilled in your young child can make the teen years either a pleasant or a challenging time.

Teaching Direction-Following Concepts to Your Child

Ti.DS

- Use the following toys, pictures, and daily home objects to enhance direction following.
    Rubber balls
    Math counters
    Large plastic eggs
    Stuffed animals
    Paper plates
    Colored construction paper
    Washable markers
    Child safe scissors
    Solid plastic people and animals
    Puzzles
    A small chalkboard or white board
    Concept books and pictures
    Picture books
    Coloring books

- Try to teach the following concepts by first grade: *whole, half, center, corner, in, out, side, right, left, bottom, top, first, last, and middle.*
- Ask the kindergarten teacher for any other concepts needed for the first grade.

Promoting Reading/Literacy Skills

Literacy

Tis

To promote early literacy skills, take your child to libraries
and bookstores.
Use simple board books that can't be tom, then advance to
picture books.
As the child's reading level increases, ask the librarians for
age-appropriate books.
Select books with audiotapes to expand independence in
elementary-age children.

Reading

Tips

- Purchase plastic alphabet letters. A magnetic board is
  helpful. The letters can be used for teaching sound
  recognition. Spell out simple words, use single
  word/picture flashcards to imitate.
- Develop your own picture/word flash cards with index
  cards, magazine pictures, and markers.
- Use phonics flashcards.
- Ask your child's teacher or librarian for ideas about
  simple computer alphabet and reading software.
- Select books at your child's reading and interest level
  to increase the joy of reading.
- Fill indot-to-dot letters and words.

- Trace alphabet letters and words.
- Tape index cards or Post-it® notes to objects in your home to promote functional reading.
- Pronounce two or more syllable words by breaking them up and saying them   slowly.
- Begin with very basic reader books from school or the library to practice at home.
- Many bookstores and learning stores are great in finding beginning reading materials.
- Less television and more reading will expand your child's literacy skills.
- Libraries and teachers can be good resources for taped phonics reading programs.

Enhancing Your Child's Gifts and Talents

Each child is an original. Look for areas that interest your particular child and help your child develop them. His or her gifts and talents may be very different from either parent's interests.

Look through the following list of strengths to see where your child shines.

- Is curious about everything.
- Has good memory skills.
- Is a leader-type child.
- Is musical.
- Sings around the house.
- Pretends everything is a drum.
- Enjoys puzzles.
- Dances every chance she can.
- Has a funny sense of humor.
- Is athletic with balls, at gymnastics, and with gym equipment.
- Completes work on time.
- Has good verbal communication skills.
- Likes his room and activities organized.
- Enjoys working with people in a variety of activities.
- Is interested in how objects are put together and operate.
- Likes building Leggo® block towers and roads.
- Enjoys drawing, coloring, or painting.

Tips

To enhance your children's gifts and talents, consider the following tips:

- Develop an art box with lots of creative objects and materials.
- Let children listen to a wide variety of music: classical, jazz, bluegrass, folk, gospel, instrumental, and music from around the world.
- Visit a music store to investigate musical instruments.
- Attend concerts with your child for a variety of music styles.
- Take field trips to museums, national landmarks, parks, factories, etc.
- Introduce computer learning programs and games.
- Let your children join clubs and groups that build character, cooperation, and respect.
- Encourage your children to participate in music, art, sports, cooking, and computer lessons, etc., to build self-discipline and self-esteem.

Tips to Help Your Child Become a Better Student

The following tips can enhance your child's performance as a student:

Tips for the Parent

- Unless your child is ill, he should be going to class. Attendance is important.
- Your child needs adequate sleep; she is still growing.
- Nutritious snacks and food are important for proper alertness and brain function.
- Make sure your child has plenty of pencils, pens, erasers, and notebook paper. Erase-type pens will help essay tests look neater.

Tips for the Child

- Look over your new textbooks (table of contents, pictures, tables, summaries, headings, and glossary).
- When reading chapters, take notes and write out vocabulary flashcards with definitions.
- Read at a correct rate to recall the main points.
- Review daily vocabulary flashcards.
- When taking tests:
    - Get plenty of rest, eat before going to the test, stay calm, and keep a clear focus.
    - Pack a snack energy bar if the test is long and there is a break scheduled.
    - Be on time to take the test; being late causes stress.

- Listen to all the directions before you start to take the test.
- Think positive thoughts: you have prepared for the test and you can do well.
- Tune out other students around you to avoid distractions.
- Write neatly and check your answers.
- Remember your first answer is probably correct, so leave it unless some information on the test tells you it's wrong.
- Don't spend too much time on one area. Pace yourself and come back to the difficult questions later.

And More . . .

- Speech/Articulation

- Vision

- Hearing

- Voice

- Fluency/Dysfluency (Stuttering)

- Talking Late

- Leaming Differences/Disabilities

- Behavior Problems

And More . . .

This final section relates specific information about speech development. Itexplains articulation delays and factors that can influence speech skills.

Vision is defined in its relationship to reading performance.

Some hearing tips are covered to help parents become more aware of warning signs for possible hearing loss.

Fluency (the rate at which we speak) and stuttering (fluency dysfunction) also are discussed in this section.

The segment about learning differences gives a concise overview of this topic and tips for parents to help their child learn more successfully.

The last topic in this section investigates behavior problems and provides useful recommendations to improve behavior.

More tips are suggested to make a positive change with these special concerns. Ifafter trying the recommendations, you find that your child is still having difficulty, be sure to seek out other professionals.

Parenting children is a learn-as-you-go experience. Itis hoped that this book will fill in the gaps and help you feel more successful in your role as your child's parent.

Speech/Articulation

As outlined in the "Birth to Twelve Years" section, speech sounds have a regular progression of development.

Children are unique in their development and may differ slightly from one another.

Factors That Can Influence or Delay Speech Skills

- Has cerebral palsy.
- Has dental overbite/underbite.
- Possesses poor motor planning from the brain to the lips, tongue, cheeks, and jaw areas.
- Imitates an older sibling who has speech errors.
- Enjoyed talking baby talk.
- Has a large tongue as in Down's Syndrome.
- Is tongue-tied (the little piece of skin under the tongue goes all the way to the end), which inhibits tongue movement.
- Wears braces. Though braces can help teeth realign in the long run, while they are on the teeth, braces can make it more difficult to speak clearly.
- Learned to talk while holding a pacifier or bottle in her mouth, which can create a clenched jaw position and a tongue-thrust movement of the tongue.
- Stuttering is evident, which reduces the child's motivation to speak.
- Thumb and finger sucking can slow articulation development by producing a tongue-thrust pattern.

Vision

During well-baby check-ups, your pediatrician will note eye appearance and basic function. Are the eyes moving or tracking? Do they have a side-moving back-and-forth problem (nystagmus), or are they crossed (one eye turned in, etc.)? **If** the pediatrician believes there is a problem, he can refer you to a doctor who is an eye specialist (ophthalmologist).

Your local school district has annual vision screenings. Ifyour child passed the screening but is still having problems, check with a local optometrist for further assessment.

Tips

The following are tips that you can look for in your child's eye performance:

- Can your child move his eyes in a coordinated manner (up and down and side to side) when you put a toy in front of his face?
- Does your child complain of headaches after reading books?
- Does she have a short visual attention span when watching television, working on the computer, reading books, or working puzzles, etc.?
- Does your child have difficulty reading road signsor board information?
- Do you notice squinting when your child is reading books, watching television, or performing computer activities?

- Does your child consistently trip and walk into things?
- Is your child having difficulty learning to read?

Vision Terms

- <u>Near sightedness:</u> The child can see close up more clearly than far away.
- <u>Far sightedness:</u> The child can see far away, but has difficulty seeing close up; this could impair reading function.
- <u>Astigmatism:</u> The vision is not clear due to the way light rays fall on the eye, which can reduce reading performance.

Hearing

Hearing within normal limits is important in speech and language development. Your child will have hearing screenings when attending school. If you suspect a hearing problem, have your pediatrician refer you to an audiologist for further testing.

Ask your pediatrician to check your child's ears for chronic middle ear fluid, a condition that can reduce hearing function.

Tis

The following list presents tips to carefully observe if you suspect that your child's hearing is impaired:

- Does your child consistently turn his head towards sounds and voices?
- Does his body show a startle response or does his facial expression change to loud noises?
- Is speech and language development delayed?
- Does her cry sound too high or too low?
- Does your child startle when you approach from the side or back positions?
- Is your child usually very quiet and doesn't talk much for his age level?
- Is she missing directions or important information in conversational speech?
- Does your child speak in a voice that is unusually high or low for his age?

Voice

Ifyou notice that your child's quality, pitch, or loudness levels are not appropriate for his age, check the following list of voice concerns:

Voice Concerns

- Speaks with a hoarse voice that doesn't change.
- Speaks in an excessively loud voice.
- There are pitch breaks.
- Often yells at sports events and during play activities.
- Volume is too soft.
- Exhibits poor breath support when speaking.
- Pitch is too high or too low.
- Has throat pain and redness due to post-nasal drip.
- Is constantly clearing his throat.

Tips

- Check with your pediatrician or a speech pathologist if these issues persist.
- Make sure enough liquids are consumed each day to adequately moisten mouth and throat areas.
- In the winter months, check to see if the bedroom air is too dry.
- Use a cool air/mist humidifier when necessary to promote moist air.

Fluency/Dysfluency (Stuttering)

Fluency is the normal rate of speech in conversation. Depending on your regional area in the country, fluency can be faster or slower.

Dysfluency or stuttering is the repeating of sounds, syllables, or whole words in conversational speech. The average person may have experienced a mild form of repeating sounds when in a very stressful speaking situation. Speech sounds can be lengthened or omitted. Some children will hesitate and replace words that are difficult with easier ones.

A speech pathologist is an important resource professional who helps reduce stuttering in children.

Tips

You as a parent can follow these tips to reduce your child's stress in speaking:

- Give your child plenty of time to get ready for preschool or elementary school.
- Let your child know of any changes in routines ahead of time.
- Make sure your child gets enough rest.
- Keep background noise distractions to a minimum.
- Wait for your child to complete his words and sentences.
- Realize that phone conversations can be stressful to dysfluent children.
- Understand that reciting parts in school and community programs can also be a stressful speaking expenence.

- Singing with a choir can help promote confidence since most children don't stutter while singing.
- A speech pathologist can work on specific activities to reduce stuttering and enhance fluency in a variety of speaking situations.

Talking Late

Why is my child late in talking? The following list contains some possibilities that could contribute to late speech and language development.

- Hearing loss
- Motor speech problems and poor coordination
- Athletic motor child; his focus is on movement.
- Developmental disability
- Cerebral palsy
- Autism
- Vocal cord paralysis
- Pronounced over-or under-bites of teeth
- Received what he wants by pointing.
- Selectively mute by choice or a traumatic event
- Others in the family are very verbal, so the child remains quiet.
- An introverted child prefers to listen and watch others.
- Tongue-tied (The little flap under the tongue is too thick and long. Pediatricians will have it clipped if they and the speech pathologist agree it is impairing speech.)
- The child has a stuttering disorder.

Tips

You can help your child talk by using the following tips:

- Speak with normal words and intonation. Baby talk delays your child's speech due to poor speech modeling.

- Give your child plenty of time to express himself.
- Initiate fun home activities and short field trips to build language and memories.
- Cut out magazine pictures, label them, and glue them to pages in a ring binder. Using plastic page sleeves will protect the pictures.
- Read simple storybooks, naming the characters, objects, and actions.
- Purchase talking toys or computer programs and books that promote word imitation. Check your school and local libraries for computer programs.
- Praise your child often for her verbal efforts.
- Supply counting and alphabet flashcards, games, books, and toys.
- Talk about the size, shape, color, texture, and function of household objects and pictures.
- Use photographs of frequently asked-for items, place them in a notebook or put them on a Velcro® board on the refrigerator. Ask, "What do you want?" after the child selects the photo. Say the word and praise the child with enthusiasm.
- Produce short carrier phrases to help enhance word production: "I want a drink." "The car is red." "Where is your shoe?" etc.
- Provide your child with simple children's audiotapes, CDs, and vocabulary story videos, which can expand vocabulary.

> A speech pathologist can screen your preschool child to see if the delay is significant enough to require further testing.

Learning Differences/Disabilities

Children are born with distinctive strengths, characteristics, and learning styles. Children who learn differently need modifications to help them absorb, process, store, and express information. There are several main learning styles; individual children can have a combination of learning styles, although there usually is a more dominant sensory mode in each child.

Types of learners:

- <u>Visual learners</u> use their eyes more when learning.

- <u>Auditory learners</u> tend to be excellent listeners and can remember something well after hearing it once.

- <u>Kinesthetic learners</u> are more touch oriented. These learners like to move around and see how things work and often have a hard time with structured-type activities (e.g., sitting at the desk).

The key to success is finding out what learning style your child demonstrates, then build skills from that point. Learning disabilities are basically defined as when a child falls behind academically in core subjects due to learning problems and differences. It takes patience to build a child's self-esteem when he can't read, spell, or perform math at the level of his classmates.

Professionals trained in reading and learning disabilities can be a valuable asset to parents for ideas in helping with skills and homework.

Tips

The following tips can be helpful for children who learn differently:

- Tape record part (main points, vocabulary, summary) or all of their textbooks.
- Teach note-taking to help organize information, increase comprehension, and build memory.
- Develop flashcards of vocabulary and definitions for each chapter.
- Reading is the foundation to learning; it is essential that children obtain strong basic reading skills.
- Check school options for extra help in reading.
- Ask your school or local library for reading and learning programs to practice at home.
- Check out library books at your child's level to promote the joy of reading.
- Make or buy phonics flashcards; say and trace the word with your child.
- Have your child spend less time with television and more time with you, reviewing flashcards, audiotapes, and books.
- Ask the classroom teacher, who is a wealth of information, to send work home for extra credit.
- Hire a private tutor to help with reading abilities.
- Investigate the Internet for more ideas to promote reading skills.

Does your child have a light-sensitivity problem? Colored transparent sheets can help. Ask a reading specialist to assess for this visual challenge.

Spelling

This academic area can be enhanced by word games, spelling toys, practice drills, alphabet letters, and computer software programs. Involving more senses, such as sight, hearing, and touch, in spelling activities promotes accuracy.

Math

Hands-on math counters, real money, math games, objects for fractions and percentages can improve math skills. Computer programs that increase ability in addition, subtraction, multiplication, and division can be purchased. Washable colored markers, pencils, and construction paper are great for learning whole, half, quarter, concepts, etc. Simple mixing and adding ingredients can help teach fractions.

Behavior Problems

Parents who see their child behaving in an inappropriate manner can ask themselves if their child exhibits certain behaviors:

- Has a temper that is easily set off.
- Doesn't obey limits or rules.
- Puts the blame on other people around him.
- Is very sensitive to words and touch.

First write down a type of checklist:

- Where does the negative behavior surface and when does it happen?
- Toward whom is it directed?
- What are the events leading up to it?
- What did the child have to eat and drink that day?
- How much sleep did the child get the night before?

A medical check-up is a good idea if you have tried various things to help your child and nothing is working well. The pediatrician can test for food allergies, mood disorders, or a variety of medical possibilities. Professional counselors, psychologists, or psychiatrists can help with the emotional aspects of the situation.

Tips

There are many things that parents can try to change their child's behavior.

- Be consistent with demands and behavior expectations.
- Reward good behavior with praise and favorite child activities.
- Keep promises to children to build trust.
- Demonstrate being a good role model in how you handle problems and disappointments.
- Find your child's strengths and gifts to build self-esteem.
- Reduce sugar, food dyes, preservatives, caffeine foods, and beverages. Some children will tantrum after consuming foods with these substances.
- Use time-outs for younger children. A timer is helpful so they can see/hear when the time is up.
- Develop a behavior/house rules sheet and post it. Review it as needed.
- Take privileges away for poor behavior. Explain what kind of behavior you expect the next time.
- Create a daily routine sheet for your child if she seems to need reminders. List activities from getting up to going to bed.
- Watch less television, reducing the number of programs and cartoons your child watches that promote violence. Do watch more educational programs.
- Investigate the music your child is listening to. Does it sound angry or stressful? Buy more calming CDs for listening enjoyment.
- To promote peaceful family times together, avoid playing the television or radio during meals.
- Serve fresher foods with fewer preservatives for proper nutrition and fewer food-related tantrums.
- Serve white or regular milk instead of chocolate milk for school-age children who act up. Chocolate milk

has a lot of sugar and caffeine. Some children may drink up to two cartons a day: one at snack time and another at lunch.

- Be sure your child gets adequate rest to avoid irritable and demanding behaviors.
- Give your child plenty of time to get ready for school. An alarm clock and watch give helpful reminders.
- Have your child take a bath or shower the night before school.
- Also pack lunches and lay out clothes and homework assignments the night before school.
- Do homework right after school or shortly after dinner. The television should be off and distractions down to a minimum. The longer homework is delayed, the greater the chances for behavior outbursts.

About the Author

Katie Marie Bille grew up in Oshkosh, Wisconsin, in a family of seven children. She is married and the mother of two daughters. Katie earned several degrees: Bachelor's of Science Degrees in Communicative Disorders, and Radio TV Film at the University of Wisconsin-Oshkosh. A Master's of Science Degree in Communicative Disorders, and Teacher Certification in Early Childhood Exceptional Educational Needs, from the University of Wisconsin-Whitewater. Courses in Continuing Education have been taken at the University of Wisconsin Cooperative Extension and from the American Speech Hearing Association in Rockville, Maryland.

Katie has more than twenty years of experience working with children and adults in urban and rural public schools, Birth to Three home programs, on an army base, at outpatient clinics, on a Native American Indian reservation, in skilled nursing facilities, and at hospitals. She also has been a traveling speech pathologist and has lived and worked in eight states.

Extensive experience and study went into writing and compiling this book. Itis the author's hope that this information will be a useful parents' reference, helping their children reach their fullest potential.

Bibliography
Great Sources for Further Reading

Anderson, R., & Miles, M. *Communicative Evaluation Chart (Birth to Three)*. Cambridge, Massachusetts: Education Publishing Service, Inc.

Barkley, Russell A., Ph.D., & Benton, Christine M. *Your Defiant Child: 8 Steps to Better Behavior*. Guilford Press. 1998.

Brazelton, T. Berry, M.D., & Sparrow, Joshua D., M.D. *Touch Points Three to six: Your Child's Emotional Behavioral Development*. Perseus Publishing. 2001.

Dodge, Diane Trister, & Bickart, Toni S. *Preschool for Parents*. Teaching Strategies, Inc. 1998.

Eisenberg, Arlene, Murkoff, Heidi E., & Hathaway, Sandra E. *What to Expect: The Toddler Years*. Workman Publishing Company, Inc. 1994.

Feldman, William, M.D. *Learning Disorders*. Firefly Books, Ltd. 2000.

Ginsberg, Erika Hoff, *Language Development*. Brooks/Cole Publishing Company. 1997.

Green, Gordon W., Jr., Ph.D., *How to Get Straight A's in School and Have Fun at the Same Time*. Thomas Doherty. 1999.

Hall, Susan L., & Moats, Louisa C., Ed.D., *Straight Talk About Reading*. Contemporary Books. 1999.

Kelly, Marguerite, *The Mother's Almanac Goes to School (Your Child From Six to Twelve)*. Doubleday. 1989.

Linksman, Ricki, *Solving Your Child's Reading Problem*. Citadel Press Books. Carol Publishing Group. 1995.

Miller, Nancy B., *Nobody's Perfect (Living & Growing With Children Who Have Special Needs)*. Paul H. Brooks Publishing Company, Inc. 1994.

Nekola, Julie, *Helping Kids With Special Needs*. Nekola Books. 2001.

Rein, RaeLynne P., & Rein, Rachel, *How to Develop Your Child's Gifts and Talents During the Elementary Years*. RGA Publishing Group, Inc. 1994.

Schor, Edward L., M.D., *The American Academy of Pediatrics: Caringfor Your School-Age Child Ages 5-12*. Bantam Books. 1995.

Index

Ordering Information

Child Development and More ...
Birth to Twelve Years

United States (includes shipping
and handling within the U.S.) **$29.50**

Canada and other countries (includes
shipping and handling) **$34.50**

Order from:
(Checks or money orders only, please)

Orange Tree Publications
P.O. Box 70
Cross Plains, WI 53528

Phone: (608) 798-0687

www.ingramcontent.com/pod-product-compliance
Lightning Source LLC
Chambersburg PA
CBHW071006040426
42443CB00007B/689